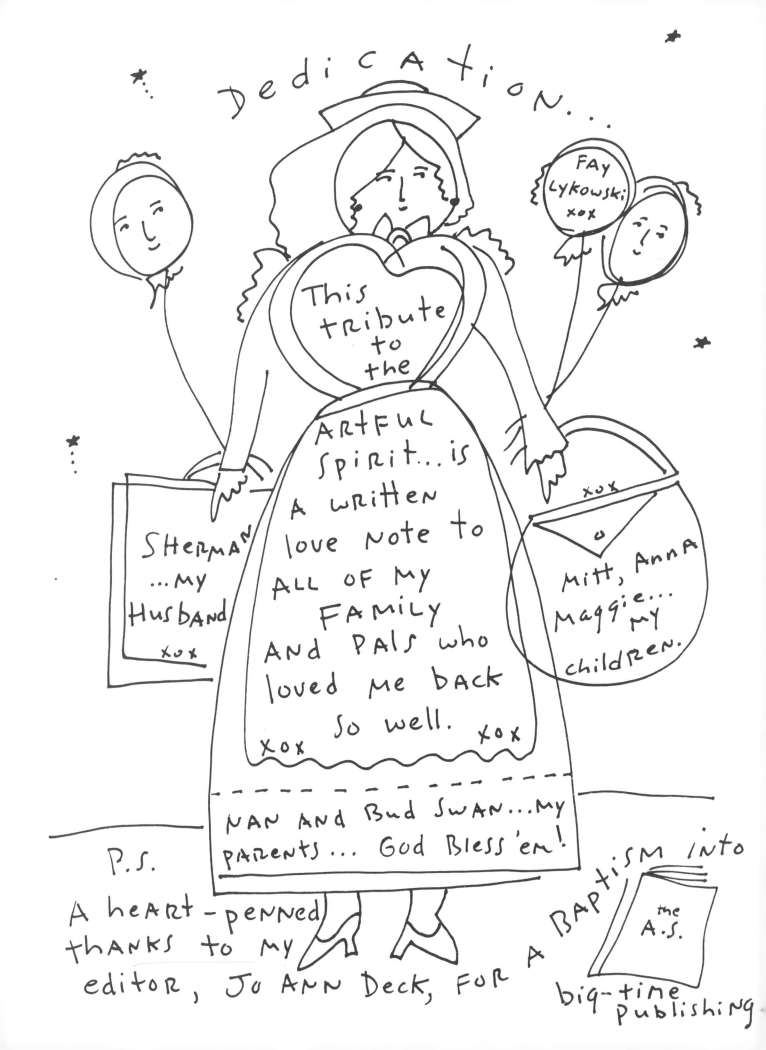

...THE ARTFUL SPIRIT...

CRAFTY Hobbies to GIFT WRAP YOUR LiFe!

BY NANCY SWAN DREW

CELESTIAL Arts

BERKELEY CALIFORNIA

CELESTIAL ARTS
P.O. Box 7123
Berkeley, California 94707

Library of Congress Cataloging in Publication Data

The Artful spirit: crafty hobbies to gift wrap your life / by Nancy Swan Drew

p. cm.
ISBN 0-89087-960-9

TT 145.74 1999
745.5 - dc21
Printed in Hong Kong

1. Handcraft
2. Hobbies
I. Title

99-29597
CIP

First Printing, 1999
123456 - 03 02 01 00 99

2.

ALL this AND MORE I know to be true.

Nancy Drew

ART is
Building something from nothing that works like a dream... ART is a primeval melody... A universally understood language of Joy, Hope, and sorrow; As necessary as shelter, Food, and clothing. P.S. Next to love... it's the best gift you can give, one that humankind owns! It can move invisible mountains and lay claim to PEACE...

3.

TABLE OF CONTENTS

I'm dreaming of an Artful Life

CRAFTY HOBBIES FOR YOU

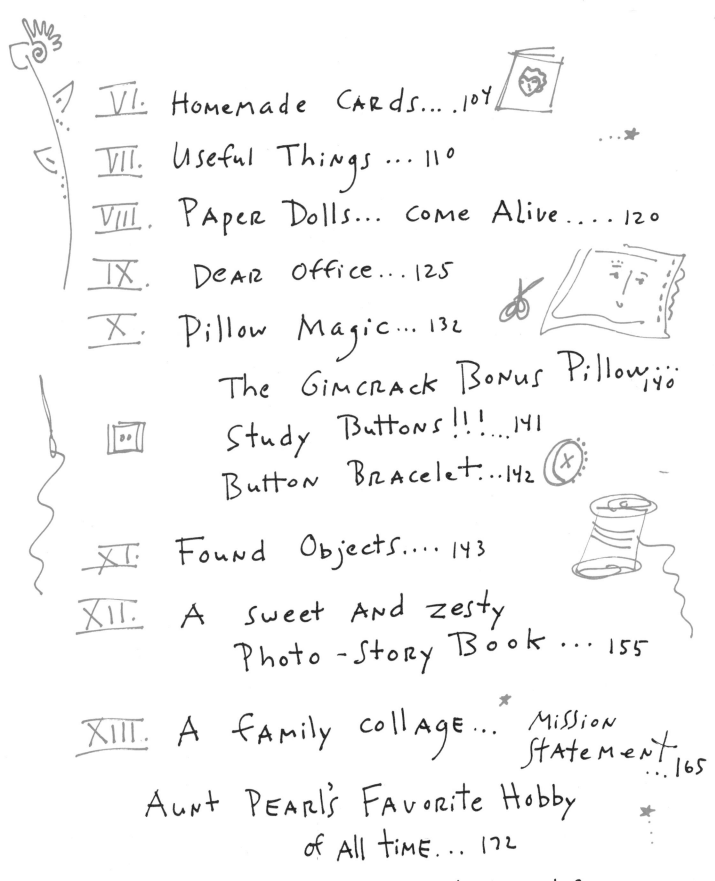

YOU ARE A FINE Hobby... DEAR ONE

LiFe's Mysterious Screenplay

Heartaches And the ARTFUL LiFe

Aunt Pearl: you, my darling, have the power to make beauty, truth, And love visible... 211

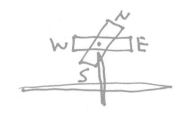

Once upon a time...
W O M E N
made beautiful, wonderful things for their nests, for themselves, And for their brood... even for their dearest friends. Very often these gifts were substitutes for pricey tokens perched

IN FANCY windows Along MAIN Street And oftentimes these substitutes were loved bAck, BIG TIMe!!

with the peARly debut of DONNA Reed, some of us MORE MODERN *(soon-to-be) women MAy have felt

SORRY for these homemade pioneers. How grand a dream it would be to order things we need and "NEED to want" from a soft throne of downy chintz.

pink princess telephone

Well, dolly, in our dream

COME TRUE _we_ hAVE been
given A cRACkERjACk
suRpRise ! ! !

Those hANdmAde dotted
swiss cuRtAiNs , smocked
dResses And decoupAged
CANistERs Atop A
R u f f l e d s h e l f gAve

these women plenty more
than what was needed.

ever so... more...

PLEASANTLY PLENTY

The crackerjack surprise
is this ... As they were
sculpting the perfect face
of a cheery cherry PIE

And cross-stitching tea towels, cozy mittens, pillowcases, aprons, and pot holders,

sweet dreams... dolly

WELCOME

their Artful Spirit was Happily Orchestrating A

Symphony of Triumph

....Triumph over the mundane laborious steps we each must take to keep our lives moving along. Some of us travelers prefer wild horses or a lipstick-red convertible to a slow, very tired SHUFFLe.

We'd rather SoAR on By!!

I have always had a beloved LiAisoN

...with CRAYONS, AND All of
their Allies... scissors, paste,
cardboard, Ribbon, paint, etc.
This relationship is most
precious to me. It has
given my Artful spirit A
full-time job... with endless
promotions, bonuses, And especially
O W N E R s h i p.

In playground terms... I
have made A zillion things with
my hands And whatever

16.

else life has given me to work with. RAIN OR SHINE. Salt or sugar. This book is A gift to all Artful spirits, No matter how Awake or still. Embolden your eyes with A MAGical SEE-through SCARF!!

I MAY color outside the lines And ignore All NAYSAyers

EMBRACE key-bearers...
those who open doors, wide!

17.

...And create Freely
so that the promise of
these pages will land like
rose petals upon your Heart.
I offer you my own Adventures,
which Assist me in my
creative trekking through this
Amazingly mazed garden...
EArth,

SORROW
FAMILY
WORLD
WORK
LOVE
JOY
PUZZLES
twisters

And crafty hobbies
to gently, exquisitely
Gift Wrap your
Life

MAY
you paint your self-
portrait
in the hallowed colors
of EACH NEW
Dawn...

...From this Book Forward!!

15.

...LOOK !!!.

SHAPES

LISTEN!

WIND

Materials

SHADOWS

SCALE

COLOR

DOO-DADS

CREATURES

explore

REFLECT   ooooooooo   your Findings...

Sherlock !!

20.

A city FIELD DAY...
Adventure I

TAKE A REAL DAY OFF to play
in the land of concrete and
steel. Awaken your senses to
the art forms around every
corner that may have been
missed before, as you HURRIED
about!!! This time NO shopping
for bargains or visits to
Vito for a new bob! (Remember,
in a full life, shortcuts are
for hairdressers.) Possess Your Time,

And spin it like a golden web
of promise... The promise is that
you will feel the bounty of
being alive... Wide awake to
the magic that dances around
your Bizeee feet 24 Hours a
day!!! That city
magic may be found in MUSEUMS:
buildings for works of Art, scientific
specimens or other objects of PERMANENT
VALUE. Look at their
facades and travel (with artful wings)
corridors of locked cases... secrets
abound in the storytelling of OUR
past!! This touring is not dull OR
spooky!

It's like dipping your toes into pools of an indigo SPRING. Study what is before you... (color · SHApes · textures). PRess closely to see the layers and precisely etched pulse of Another's hand, driven by A heart... Not unlike yours!! 1820 1998 Keep A small NotePAd to Assist your memory later, As you will wish to Record your discoveries!! Also visit the museum gift shops... They Are keen collectors of keepsakes to take home.. (PostCARds Are great tokens!)

While you walk the city streets, let your eyes MicRoscopically survey the grand whole and its

singular pearls of beauty:
→ decorative finials

→ slate roofing

→ Copper

IRon gates... Fencing!

glazed tiles

leaded glass

paving bricks

tight landscaping!

☆ Look for SHADOWS... different SHAPES... Fountains, Window boxes... Spectacular DOORS.

→ carved stone

cobblestone
→ WALKWAYS

sculpture

MODERN glass, MARBLE, chrome, BRASS, And tin

☆ →

shadow

LAKES??

LOOK so hard And carefully that you even Notice the key holes and door knobs!!

Well done, dolly... Now take tea time at a cozy or FANCY spot.

High tea is best... and often served at 20 ✳ STAR hotels... Try crumpets, lemon curd, salmon and watercress and cucumber sandwiches so petite Thumbelina would be proud!! Silver, white linens, and china that is roundishly sassy is what you deserve today. While you sip... glance at the company you keep and FEEL through their eyes, crisply pressed suits, and aproned uniforms, that very same pulse you came upon at the museums, those altars of PERMANENT HUMAN VALUE.

P.S. Listen to sounds... the wind, chatter, engines, and sirens. Look at the "costumes" all about. (FOR SOME, HALLOWEEN IS A daily celebration.)

City Field Day... List ☑

☐ MUSEUM OR GALLERY FINDS...

☐ City streets... Architecture and decorative appointments (shapes... materials, etc.)

☐ TEA✳time! The Human spirit outside of the museum!!

☐ EXTRA details your microscope loved!! (sounds... flowers...)

Let A new vision... make life AN adventure!

A
Country Powwow..
Adventure II

Clear a day ASAP for a date
with "MAMA" Nature,

★ For this is really a sister or
non-identical twin to your City
Field Day! Like the old tale of
the city mouse longing for the

★ country and the country mouse pining
for the skyscrapers, our creative
blueprints are best drafted with
a bit of both lands. So... pack a
camera, a picnic of thoughtful foods (no
drive-thru!! tsk-tsk), a blank

journal, camp blanket... Windham Hill sounds to pop in your auto. RelAx as your rearview mirror shrinks the city into a tabletop whatnot and You Find A "still" spot affording her very best gifts... A river, lake, meadow, or sandy dune... As sure as Butterflies FLY carrying you to her Majesty. FORGet About Everything For now... darlin... for now.

Plant your Artful spirit in the heart of the most loving, Authentic cathedral on earth... under a stand of pines or atop a beach that talks one lap at a time. Begin this encounter by

Resting flat on your back... like that child who once made snow angels full-time. Watch the merry-go-round of clouds above you. Inhale the perfumes that cannot be bottled, listen to little nations of creatures talking to one another... Are they sharing a peace treaty or planning a global picnic?? Hush now...

Next... take a walk under this canopy! Find the horizon line and follow its ribbon of color, shapes, and shades of light until you bring your "binoculars" closer to what is beside you.

Feel what is underfoot... moss, pebbles... sand?? Are there tracks from wild turkeys or (ooops) dirt bikes? Are the trees beside you "uncles" or "grandmothers" or "newborns"? What does their bark and posture tell you?

Take your picnic at last... scribe your notes, DRAW WHAT YOU SEE!!! Before you head back, gather a few mementos (a feather or stone or piece of birch bark) and of course your THoughts. Even... snapshots for your desk. Paste one here.

Country Powwow
List ☑

🦇 Sights

🦇 Sounds

🦇 Perfumes

🦇 Textures

🦇 Colors

🦇 Shapes

Secret thoughts... dreams, Hopeful
Questions, And ... mmm.. ★

How do you grade your "conference"?? [A+]

??

31.

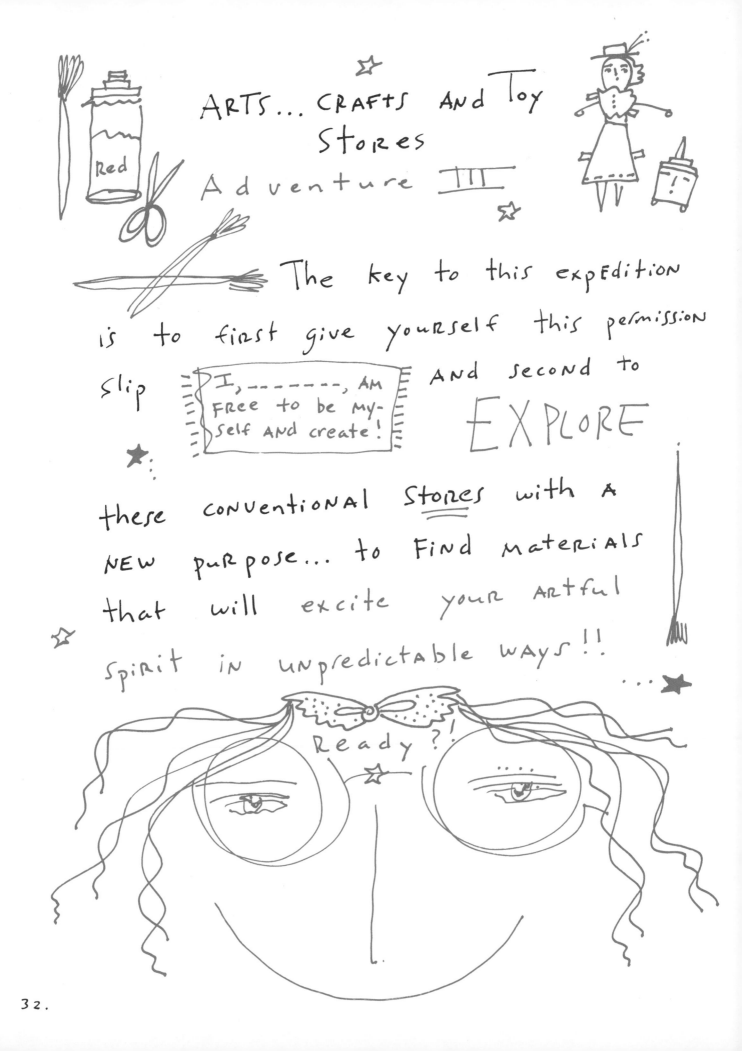

ARTS... CRAFTS AND Toy
Stores
Adventure III

The key to this expedition
is to first give yourself this permission
slip   I, _____, AM
       Free to be My-
       self And create!   And second to
EXPLORE

these conventional Stores with A
NEW purpose... to Find materials
that will excite your Artful
spirit in unpredictable Ways!!

Ready?!

Red

The Art store is a grown-up coloring box! Full of tools to tell stories with... looking for your voice!! Ask for help in understanding these tools... Do not let fancy words stall your imagination. There is no private club of artistes... Membership is free to one and all!

★ Look for exquisite Japanese papers (find them in drawers or boxes), English inks, self-hardening clays, soapstones with carving tools. Collect now and decide later how your free will shapes their fate, dolly! xox

Next, enter the world of an American craft store... it can be HUGE or a local five and dime icon or an updated VARIETY store. Walk each aisle slowly... like rowing a canoe down a gentle stream. Take care to see the beauty of its ...★ L A N d s c a p e. ★

You will see wooden balls, shelves, Styrofoam, simple glass plates, and paints that will stay put even in the dishwasher, stencils... decals!! Again... fill your cart as you so wish!! Take a deep breath and feel the invisible... Awaiting debut! ★

Finally the toy store... Hallelujah! Shelf after shelf of candy colors and trinkets that cry, "PLAY all day... the blues will wait until tomorrow!" As you see these modern-day gizmos and "Must Haves", recall those memories that will help you find the "toys" that survive still: Pot holder kits... those made of weaving loops on a hand-held loom in checkerboard fashion! Etch-A-Sketch for doodling... eternally! Colorforms, Play-Doh, Silly Putty, and a new product/FUN-FOAM/await your vision, too! Somewhere in

this August place there are little
shelves of trinkets... glass marbles,
dominoes, plastic people, frogs,
perhaps canceled stamps from foreign
lands... Odd wonders that belong
in your Repertoire of Future
concerts that will bring you and
others unspeakable joy. Go ON
Now... tuck them into your cart...
No one will dare to ask if these
are for Nephews or nieces, and if
they do, smile and say, "Absolutely
Not... they are for my Artful SELF!"
                    Once you return home...
steep a pot of sweet tea and

peruse your bounty. DIAl A public Radio station on the TALK-Box and perhaps weave up A Nice fresh batch of potholders in Picasso's favorite Red-yellow-And-Black motif or AN "I Love Lucy" pink And lavender!!! DARe to doodle or use the silly Putty to mirror the cartoons in today's paper. Just PLAY A Little Bit, dolly!!!

xox

P.S. your ARtFuL spirit is dE-lighted 200%.

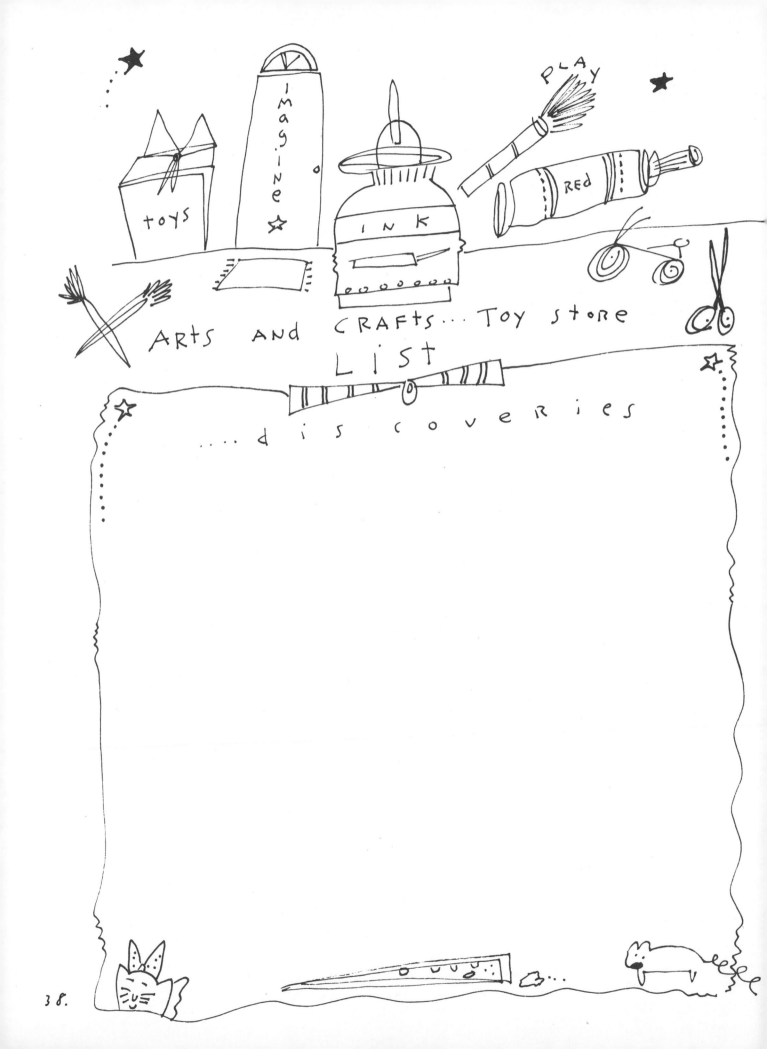

Arts and Crafts...Toy store

List

...discoveries

39.

The trusty Hardware store Adventure IV.....

SOMEtimes the best darn surprises in life ARE discovering the unexplored talents of objects that pretend to be <u>solitary</u> souls. Like the softer BEAuty that lies within the ugly duckling's white feathery cloak, so it is true of "<u>things</u>". ^{e.g.} A stiff sisal rope for hauling, binding, and linking CAN shine AS A cording to hang drapes Atop A window!!

The Hardware store offers a practical museum of man's inventions... just awaiting FREEDOM to tap-dance a new tune. Imagine this scene at night when all contractors are resting at home over a nice MEATLOAF supper... with wife and kiddos.

Hank's
Hardware
est. 1897

bippety bop

dA-BOP

diddy... DOE

Gosh... we wish an ARTFuL spirit would come to shop!

So let THE Adventure begin!
Take a long glance at what sits
dutifully in little drawers and boxes,
what is rolled in tight balls and
what dangles from the mighty hooks
of your very own "Hank's Hardware"
when you encounter each gadget
and gizmo... X-RAY to see other possibilities. FOR EXAMPLE.. at our
small cottage down south there were
many finials along an upper deck...
plainly, geometrically HANDsome.

3-D
finial

bEach

Their purpose was to enhance the eye's 👀 visit to our abode, as they pointed skyward. However... to me on a rainy afternoon they looked like they could use mmm... a little HOUSE- JEWELRY Not to be found at Tiffany's... no MA'AM, but at the Hardware store. Look what caught my eye!!

silver galvanized electric plate

copper clip

for this spot

steel water faucet handle

steel ← → white plastic

→ doodad perhaps a pulley

FOR this center

lovely COPPER nails

With these trinkets the FINIALS were finally dressed.

43.

HARDWARE LIST....

P.S. How about a metal FLue cover?!
A perfect surface for a PORTRAit!

The Bizee Flea Market
AND 2nd HAND Store
Adventure V

These places might be the most authentic museums on earth because they give us all of culture without a satin-glove presentation and allow us regular FOLKS to touch things, junk and trash included. The "permanent value" of these collections can be argued, I suppose, except, dolly, the only real things of permanent value have never been seen... only felt or known to be true.

I remember a time, many years ago, when our younger family refurbished a "wrecker's ball" shack. A fancy woman of high place stopped by to witness this face-lift, which, of course, included many dusty, sleepy flea-market finds. Her face told me clearly what her words did not say... "Where do you find THESE things, Nancy dear?" Well, happy to say, not at Neiman's or Bloomingdale's. I really think soap and water, silver polish, and needle wed to Mr. thread can doll up the ARTFUL spirit's best work. Unfortunately, her disposition preferred the safe lands of Judgment,

...where the sunsets are black and the sunrises white. Do not let this happen to you, doll-face! MERcy me! Like a happy, non-stuck-up sleuth, let your eyes go to town at these spots of wonder. Look for the testimonials of everyday miracles... A pincushion made out of a tuna fish can covered in felts and ribbon... A CROSS of hope made from dyed-in-tea matchsticks... A cigar box covered in tiny pink seashells... camp stools fashioned from hickory logs and woolen blankets. Utilitarian blue-ribbon winners!! Gather ideas and goood prospects!! xox

47.

SHOPPING

THRIFTY FEVER LIST.....

THE GROCERY
Adventure VI

$ $

This is a revolutionary trip for your errand-running soul... Push a cart, aisle by aisle, and with your wide eyes study the _colors_, _shapes_, and _textures_ of PRODUCTS. Please!! No shopping, dolly!

Fill with images only

Take candid-camera shots with all of your SENSES of the "Fellowship of Shoppers" that meets faithfully at the checkout!! One by one, study their eyes and hear their voices. Perhaps you will see yourself... the weary mother with child or the sassy, single "chickie-babe" on a mission, or the demure grandmother examining the sodium content of what she once loved without a blink. Squint your vision long enough to see AN abstract Ribbon of ENERgy... Then, open your EYES in A most certain search for PRIZE-winners... A box, can, or plastic - wrapped satchel that calls you near. Record your selections on the next page!! IN any given moment, your ARTful net-work can shower itself with quiet moonbeams... EVEN while Fetching milk At the grocery.

GROCERY RIBBON
WINNERS

First PLACE... BLUE RIBBON!
PACKAGING!

Second PLACE... PINK RIBBON!
CANNED Goods!

Third PLACE... Green RIBBON!
CHARACTERS!!!

Fourth PLACE... ORANGE RIBBON!
CONVERSATIONAL Wit!

Fifth PLACE... Yellow RIBBON!
AROMAS!

Signage PRIZE?!!!

P.S.
Visit
SPECIALTY 11
SHOPS..

Aunt Pearl's Best Tip
For KEEN Adventures....

DEAR ONE...
    Like a five-year-old who is
Not Afraid to see the world
upside down and Inside Out..... Let
your grown-up eyes dare to
linger, seldom blinking, And once again
PRIMA facie (at first blush) those
daily paths of task and play
will lend your Artful spirit
        A NEW PERSPICACITY !!!
            Love, Aunt P. xoxo

dance laugh

build make invent

jump skip color sing

I'M
dreaming
OF
AN...

ARTFUL
LIFE

97 N. Drew

HUM

BUILD
A
DARN Good Creative NEST

VERY important, indeed, is A
spot... No matter the size, darlin,
where one can "Alight" to actually
create! A sanctuary, really. Think
about all of the other spots you
live within that have been designated
for specific purposes! My least
favorite is the → Laundry ROOM

out OF soap ?

Artful living flows within You
And of course travels freely... every-
where one wishes to go! Still,
this notion of a special nest is
a must. Imagine it being a
PERSONAL FULL-SERVICE FUEL STATION.
Indoors..... Assess the possibilities!
(If your home is a microscopic
apartment, play with a corner shelf!!)
Attics are grand because they tickle
the sky... Nooks and crannies
are natural cocooning shelters...
and open lofts, too, have their own
spark of wide-open prairies...
very symbolic of your imagination's

OPEN VISTAS! If a singular encapsulated space is iffy... Rely on decorative screens, drapes, or old doors (secured) as territorial barriers. Build simply...

in order to define and indulge your NEST... Be greedy!

♪ Include both soft and direct lighting, musical scores ♫, a gypsy's tonic of color... windows! Consider creating a faux window; bring in a RELIC... curtain it

up a bit and perhaps place a
printed picture behind it, or actually
paint your own vision!

Voilà!!

Remember a plump-comfy chair
to dream in... A work-play
table! NO PHONE, FAX, TV, or compu-
ter, PLeeez!! Lots of Books and
meaningful gimcracks that

stir the eye and razzle-dazzle a creative nesting. Surely include memory pieces that chart the map of your life... so FAR, that is!!

If you have the added luxury of an out-of-doors spot, you are in LUCK!! weather permitting, contrive a shelter in the form of a tent, cabin, open canopy, or shed, or simply place a camp blanket beside a stand of trees... plant a bed of wild flowers and roses to keep you company!! Know that Ms. Mother Nature is the Prima Donna of DECORATING... And you will Need to do little fussing. Look outwards when in your open-air Addendum... and take only what you need to do your work. LEAVE the wants and worries elsewhere OH, it will Feel so wonderful And "pay" you well... over And over again. I promise.

For all of your upcoming Adventures, A CREATIVE Treasury is Needed. The things that

will come to Rest in this box
aRe practical tools. Some you
may already have; others might
have been collected during your
Adventures.... And there

aRe NEW ONES to come... unimagined...
LAteR!! They CAN be accrued
over time... Not in A "bewitched"
instant.

...TURTLES ARRiVE   UNHURRIED

61.

THE ART
treasury

- Lots of colored felt-tip pens!
- Black markers... different points!
- Many papers... colored, plain, etc.
- Empty journals... lined or not!
- Self-hardening "clay" or the like.
- Acrylic paints... water based.
- Watercolors... assorted brushes.
- Nice big box... your treasury!

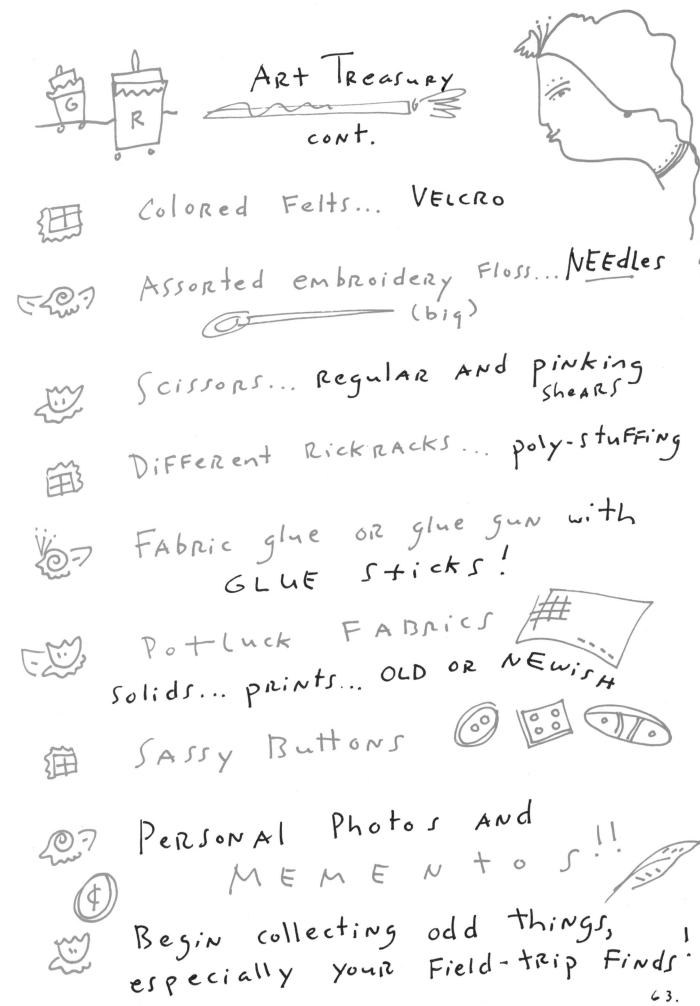

Art Treasury
cont.

Colored Felts... Velcro

Assorted embroidery floss... Needles (big)

Scissors... Regular and pinking shears

Different Rickracks... poly-stuffing

Fabric glue or glue gun with GLUE sticks!

Potluck FABRICS
solids... prints... OLD or NEWISH

Sassy Buttons

Personal Photos and MEMENTOS!!

Begin collecting odd things, especially your Field-trip Finds!

Things
I search for... like a sleuth...

Old and new Buttons, trims, LAMPS,

Antique Photo-Pins, sewing cards
of needles or buttons... souvenirs,

cocktail stir-sticks, postcards,
coasters, theatre bills... hand-pen-
ned letters or documents... wooden
& pennies... miniature flags, scraps
of vintage quilts, coverlets, and
drapery. Infant gloves... mittens.

Advertising ware... pens, calendars...
old valentines, greeting or calling
cards... sheet music + magazines...

Costume jewelry... especially enameled and rhinestone, or of plastic, wood, and crystal!

Boxes... cigar, paper, tin... wood (toothpicks, popsicle sticks). tramp art... prison art (woven from cigarette packages)!

Glass marbles, serving trays (all kinds!), enameled washing basins... FRAMES... lightning-rod glass balls, old doors, and windows!

Chairs, benches, stools... shelving and hanging racks... screens for dividing spaces... All sizes!!

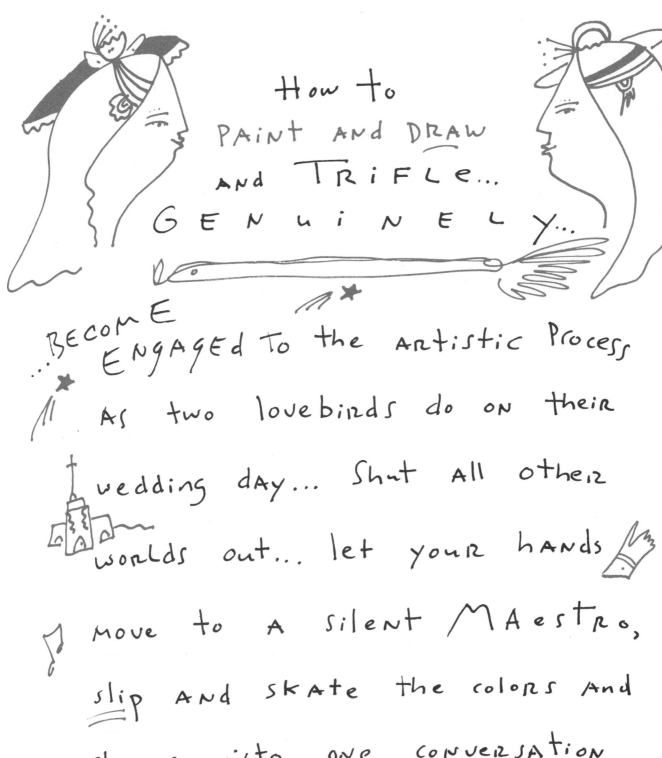

How to
PAINT AND DRAW
and TRIFLE...
GENUINELY...

...BECOME ENGAGED To the Artistic Process

As two lovebirds do on their

wedding day... Shut All other

worlds out... let your hands

move to A silent MAestro,

slip And skate the colors And

shapes into one conversation...

Discount All other opinions

And REVEL in your PRIVATE
...MiRAcle!

Aunt Pearl Says...

★ HOBBIES ★

ARE

very, <u>very</u> good For you. Because they allow you to LOVE the <u>world</u> your <u>soul</u>

knows better than <u>best</u>.

Let your Artful Spirit go on a <u>generous</u> holiday !! and

Hobby - it - Up !!!!

Hobby I

YOUR DREAM DOLLY!!

This is a very old-fashioned remedy for any kind of blues.... All shades! Play a little Judy Garland and collect these gems...

- ☆ Fabrics... vintage, Felts! Pink, Brown, or Black for Flesh side! Ribbons, Rickracks.... Stuffing.   xox

- ☆ Antique and New buttons... Satin rosettes... metal forms for making covered buttons, too!!

- ☆ Pinking shears, scissors, needle, thread, sewing machine, glue gun, glue sticks, black-ink pen...pattern-making paper.   TEA!!!

Made with loving Hands And A FRONTIER Spirit....

DReam Dolly!!!

P.S. She is much Sweeter than She looks!!

Your DReams

P.P.S. Sometimes Seeing is Remembering.

Such A Nice New PAL FoR Your SoFA!!

69.

Set your sights on fashion-ing a one-of-a-kind Doll... from scratch... that will carry your dreams, secrets and all!

Begin by drawing Free-Hand her pattern... think in terms of a full Rag doll or Gingerbread shape... cut in one piece!

★ Front is Flesh!

★ Back is Felt!

Stitch joints shut, for bending!

→ sew together on <u>top</u>!

Head And center, stuff Last!

→ use pinking shears to cut

Leave side open... close... when Finished (whipstitch)))))

★ Size! 32" Long... Hand to Hand 16" wide

LoveRly!!

Use pinking shears to cut form in flesh color and back-side materials. (I love these combinations: pink doll with black, gray, or chocolate brown felt back / black or brown doll with cobalt blue, red, or buttercup yellow felt back!) Sew or construct by machine or hand... Stuff as you wish... soft, medium, or sturdy!!!

For the DRESS... draw a simple "Frock" shape over the pattern on another piece of paper. Leave at least 3"-4" all around... See!

DO NOT WORK FOR PERFECTION... WORK FOR LOVE...

sweet LOVE

★ If you are a veteran seamstress, utilize your hard-earned tricks...

★ If you are that wide-eyed Girl (or woman) Scout trying to earn her arts and crafts badge,

A+C.

RELAX and rely on primary skills with needle, thread, and glue

★ gun... THIS Route will never fail you!!

DRESS!

trims ←

→ buttons, roses

select Fabric with character ←

→ RICKRACK

→ scallop your hem!

BACK —
close at neck with a slit... use Velcro!

FACE!

DRAW with black pen or "wite-out"

OR
stitch

Rhinestone or baby blue buttons →

Ruby Red button! →

Find worthy buttons

72.

★ Your Dream Dolly can Also be
fitted for a wardrobe At any
children's store... try a toddler's
Two. With this Approach you may
simply embellish or "Fuss" with a
★ Ready - made garment!
          For her Hairdo.... is
she a "posy-gal" or "tough-cookie"...
Rosettes or Buttons ?!?

A
Corn
Flower
look

BACK
OF
HEAD

wonderful!

Fill generously, if gluing... work
slowly! It's fine if the felt is
exposed. Now... DRAW on her
front side! Even Atop her heart!

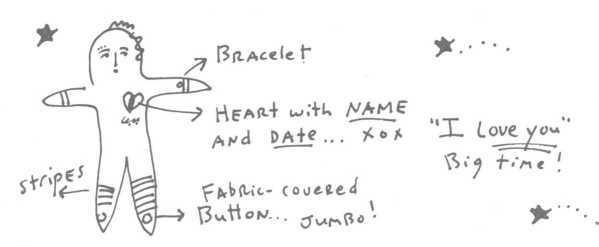

Bracelet

Heart with NAME and DATE... xox

"I love you" Big time!

stripes

Fabric-covered Button... Jumbo!

Finally... create a felt envelope, just the right size for her to carry... tie with a ribbon upon wrist.

prize button

pinked edges

close with Velcro

Then, darlin, script your dreams and tuck inside... Feel Butterfly Free to Edit as the clock Tick-tocks.

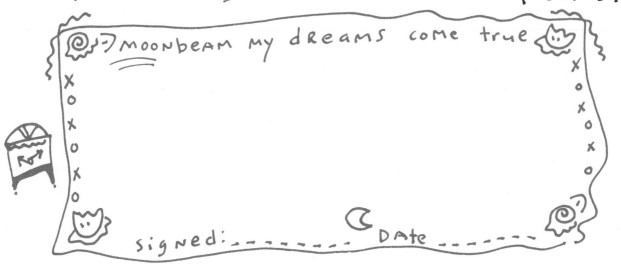

moonbeam my dreams come true

X o x o x o

x o x o x o x o

signed: _____ Date _____

Hobby II

Your Automobile
Journal

Leave any dishes in the
sink a few moments longer and
Retreat to your creative nest!
Those dishes will not demand
therapy later on... or blame you
for tardy sudsing!

xox Gather a plain journal
and the supplies you wish to
play with from your Art
Treasury. Begin decorating the
cover... perhaps with a lovely

SNAPShot of you in grade school or as a costumed Angel for Halloween?! Let the cover MIRROR your oh-so-young ARTFul Spirit!! CARRy your memory back to a time of graham crackers and a NEW box of crayons. Add words to match the HEART'S DESIRE so clearly seen in your wee eyes. Those eyes today are windows to A wiser soul, P E R H A P S.

They still, however, must have

R E C E S S...

in order to carry on!!

Auto journal

Feed your "promise" daily

☆ Recess : A suspension of business
or procedure often for
rest or RELAXation
— Webster's

Sooo, darling, while you

are suspended in your AUTO,

spend those FLOATING moments
while awaiting children, traffic,
or a Ferryboat bridge to
open and close ... within a
personal conversation of sorts!
Record ideas, wishes, questions,
observations, and Feelings during
this Adult Recess!! Keep
the tally in your glove com-
partment and as time Fast-
Forwards... REREAD!! Try not
to use this podium as a pulpit

FoR LECTURES oR TASKS
to Do!! There is enough of that
in your life!!! FoR Now, dolly,
script Away... And swing so High

that your grown-up toes touch
the sky... just A little bit, once
more. R e m e m b e r ....
up... d o w n... up... d o w n...
BENd And Kick!

Example Page... Auto Journal

time: 3:10 pm
winter, JAN 26th 1984

place: St. Mary's school parking Lot

Beyond today's steely gray and frosty face I remember the summers of "Lakeside-Heaven". Long afternoons at Elmer and Jane's beach. The three children passionately worked at digging holes to China, made cities out of clay and speckled rocks while picnicking well with hard-boiled eggs and three-layered chocolate cake. Sometimes we would forget knives and forks. At day's end, the large cottage sink in the kitchen served "just right" as a bathing tub... bubbles and all.

soap

81.

Hobby III

The Low-Maintenance FishBowl

Humor, doll-face, can take you anywhere... Far away from the blues and gray flannels of MR. WORRY!! It can unruffle feathers and calm a potential WAR into a whisper of compromise. This hobby is designed to kiss any gloom and doom Adieu!!

All you will need is a nice classic FishBowl and paints!

If you are a bit nervous, DON'T BE!

★ I suggest relaxing your hands by opening and closing... stretch! And also clapping them with vigor. Play the <u>Will Rogers</u> <u>Follies</u>, too!! Very snappy and MERRY! Looook... on the outside.

BRAVO!

PAINT A GULF OF MEXICO SCENE!! Then....

I LOVE MY VIEW!

?? ?

MMM...

gold!

AQSA

S E A S i d e ....

85.

NExt...

Add Actual sand And Real trinkets And colored WAteR!! Place youR sassy little ARt piece in the FoyeR... with An Actual box of premium FiSH Food At its side. Feel FRee to scRibe messAges Atop the glass; these can be Windexed off And changed easily (use a black felt-tip pen). Pretend Fish can be moody, too!!!!

welcome
dolly

sometimes the primary Function of a work of Art... HANDMADE is to sit in full VIEW, AS AN EVER PRESENT Witness to your Artful spirit.... Reminding you to CARRY ON CREAtively in all things Large and small.

x o x

Hobby. IV
s w e e t
Memory Pieces!!!

BACK in the 1800s, A popular
Hobby was to gather broken
bits of CHINA, silver, glass, and
odd trinkets of lore for the
purpose of cloaking an ordinary vessel, perhaps a glass
jar or cigar box. Sometimes,
the entire piece was painted
a golden tone to slightly dis-
guise its solitary fragments.
Today this is A

FL.

most suitable hobby for our

consumer - driven age. Along-

side the chipped teacups and

aunt Ivy's hat pin... can sit

a ticket stub from Les

Miserables on the Bulls

game. ★ You will need, dolly:

GLASS JARS, VASES... HAT / CIGAR

boxes... Large picture Frame

(smaller table-size also),

★ Mementos, trinkets... glue

gun, pens,   .paint !!

MIRROR

1984.
Dec 24
Shubert

82.

I especially love to mix those scraps of personal history with beautiful buttons, classic black-and-white postcards of places I've never been, and foreign canceled stamps. These age-traveled tattlers link my current spell here with the past... and remind me of the relentlessness of A collector's PASSION... AND ARTFUL SPIRIT.

OMENA Michigan

AdARe IRELAND

SEASiDE FLA.

London

88.

. . . o t h e r

knicky - knack
examples:

old matchboxes, paper coasters,
costume jewelry, shoe clips, hair
curlers (metal perm-rods), bottle
tops, button cards, souvenir pens
or pencils, broken figurines, poker
chips, playing cards, photos....
dominoes... pocket CHANGE ¢¢¢

This is a perfecto time to
clean drawers, closets... even the
family auto!! Oh yes... and
do you have a bounty of
odds and ends from your
flea market adventure ???

EVE IN PARIS

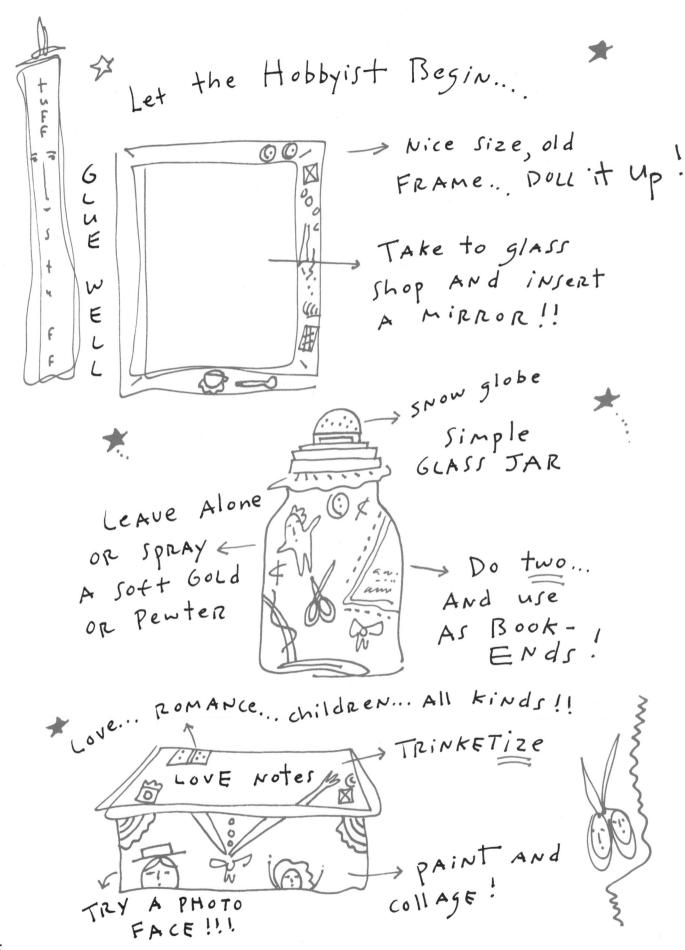

Let the Hobbyist Begin...

tuff ([...] stuff ff

GLUE WELL

→ Nice size, old FRAME... DOLL it Up!

→ Take to glass shop AND insert A MIRROR!!

→ snow globe

Simple GLASS JAR

LEAVE Alone OR SPRAY ← A soft Gold OR Pewter

→ Do two... AND use As BOOK-ENDS!

LOVE... ROMANCE... children... All kinds!!

LOVE notes

→ TRINKETize

→ PAINT AND COLLAGE!

TRY A PHOTO FACE!!!

☆ Bonus Hobby ★

for the "PERSONAL HISTORIAN"!!

Take a basic SHADOW Box from your local craft store or make your own. Select an individual or Family theme...

★ Embellish with meaningful trifles...

RUSSELL ISLAND Summers with Aunt PEARL...

pine sprig

use A sweet gingham background

her spectacles

glassine or clear envelope of SAND from the Beach

Bob

☆

glue SEAshells AND Mother-of-pearl Buttons Along deep Sides

TINA

Ferry-Boat ¢

Awning swatch

miniature Root Beer to symbolize pop stand

† Mass Card

R.B.

...xox...

Creating these very personal
shadow boxes is a joy... They
serve your heart's journey
far better than disparate
photos, etc., that sit in dark
dresser drawers amidst birth
certificates, passports, and tax
papers. Consider devoting a
corridor... that connects your
sweet family's comings and
goings... to memory pieces!!!
Also... they are gifts that
pale the retail moon above every
MALL.

92.

MEMORY PIECES....

beads, china fragments, brooches,
photos... bottle caps.... personal
KEEPSAKES
that
love you
back...
in goood
company!

glue

MERCY

Admit
ONE
2 PM

13.

Hobby V

Pet Gallery And Gifts of
Fondness !!

My true confession is that
since having A TIFF with A
RUFF-RUFF
frazzled puppy on the Rectory
steps at Age seven, I have
been what some call A "Non-
pet person".... Until recent years,
when our one-eyed dog, Tip,
And black bear of A LAB,
Jordan, came to soften this
Angst. My husband, Sherman,
is very much A "pet person"

and I do believe if dogs could smoke cigars and negotiate contracts, Jordan just might "WAg" home a paycheck.

pets Rock

J.

73

some of US ARE Nicer thAN PEOPLE

FOR THIS LOVING Hobby you will Need.... pinking shears...

Handsome wicker BED or bAsket

colorful Felts... glue gun, collar

Embroidery Floss... Needle

Glitter paint... jingle bells

FlANnel plaid pillowcases

Pictures of ANimals... bANdANNa ... RickRACk

Begin by cutting shapes of felt with pinking shears... then embroider simple designs such as X's and O's, or using paint tubes, draw a design directly onto felts! Feel free to script words as well. Glue these Hobo-type patches along the outside and inside of the pet's wicker nest... Add jingle bells here and there. Tie in a RickRack Bow!

WOOF MEOW

XOX MAMA LOVES YOU

R

POOCH

FOR MOI?

LOVE IT!

FOR the cushion, select sporty
plaid pillowcases in a soft
flannel. Close extra fabric with
velcro   or purchase
yardage to make-do a
cover that fits!! Scatter
a few of your felt patches
atop this plaid (machine-stitch or
whipstitch). Design two or
three!!
          ...Now turn your artful
spirit toward the gallery of
PET-HEAVEN!! Find magazine

MEOW

pictures or actual snapshots of friends in the ANIMAL Kingdom... Pop into Plexiglas frames or tack to a cork strip and let them dangle... At your PET'S EYE LEVEL! If you are at work all day... Add a few "family" photos of COMFORT. Finally... spruce up the BANDANA and collar to match your PET'S CHIC DOMAIN...

LASSIE'S Brother Pete

paint or stitch!

bells

→ RICK. RACK

Felts

Bonus

Hobbies for Pet Lovers...

☆ Doll up an old or new mirror and hang low to the floor... horizontally... Paint in a border that flows onto the glass in a palette of bright colors or muted tones. Create the illusion of the out-of-doors... Try a collage of a few actual pictures to give credence to this fanciful illusion.

For those who Adore their pets... often more than blood relatives, the prospect of A "PET-PHOTO TRIBUTE" in the form of an Album is A gooood Hobby. This CAN include All of the pets that lived by your side in PURR-FECT HARMONY! IN addition to photographs... include snippets of your memory's best-Kept TAILS!!!

ELLiot

1986
A dAY
At
the
FARMERS
MArket
And
BAit
SHop

it WAS
very
Hot
And...

Benny 1960-1975
Eloise 1975-1981
Ginger 1977-1984
"I LOVE you
ALL"

Another snappy idea is to visit one of those "Paint your own Pottery" spots... in order to create a lovingly practical BANQUET DISH......

...OR FANCY up A set of photo-notes At the local print shop! Take Actual pictures And scribe messages directly on top or inside.

Finally... FOR A MAJOR Hobby...
Re-invent AN older (OR Newish)
folding SCREEN <u>With</u> lots of
SNApshots and A collage
of mother Nature's best profiles!

Add
pressed
Flowers

PEts
Rule

Try
National
<u>Geographic</u>
MAGAzines!

... LOVERLY HOMEMADE CARDS

MOM
I Love YA
① Big time ②

SAIL AWAY WITH MY HEART
① A S A P ②

YOU ARE MY BEST PAL
① Forever ②

ROSES ARE PINK AND VIOLETS ARE ... SWELL
① ... HOWEVER

YOU!!! ARE MY FAVORITE GARDEN... to Love so well.
②

xox

Hobby VI

HOMEMADE CARDS!
stock up...

You will need from your
ART TREASURY: *Papers, scissors,
glue, stickers, stamps, Needle,
embroidery floss, photos!! Now
contemplate those pals, love-
mates, And Relatives to whom
you wish to express the
contours of your Heart.
List them with appropriate

Dates for contact on your
Important CARD Roster!!

Important CARd Roster

NAME   REASON   Time

CONNecting with personal CONFection

Before you begin, Allow me to share a secret... All of the most exquisitely fashioned cards on this globe of HIGH $ Commerce cannot compare to honestly scribed Feelings And Drawings FROM you!! This Hobby will Free your Artful spirit And bring Authentic JUBILAtion.

★ EXAMples, DArliN...

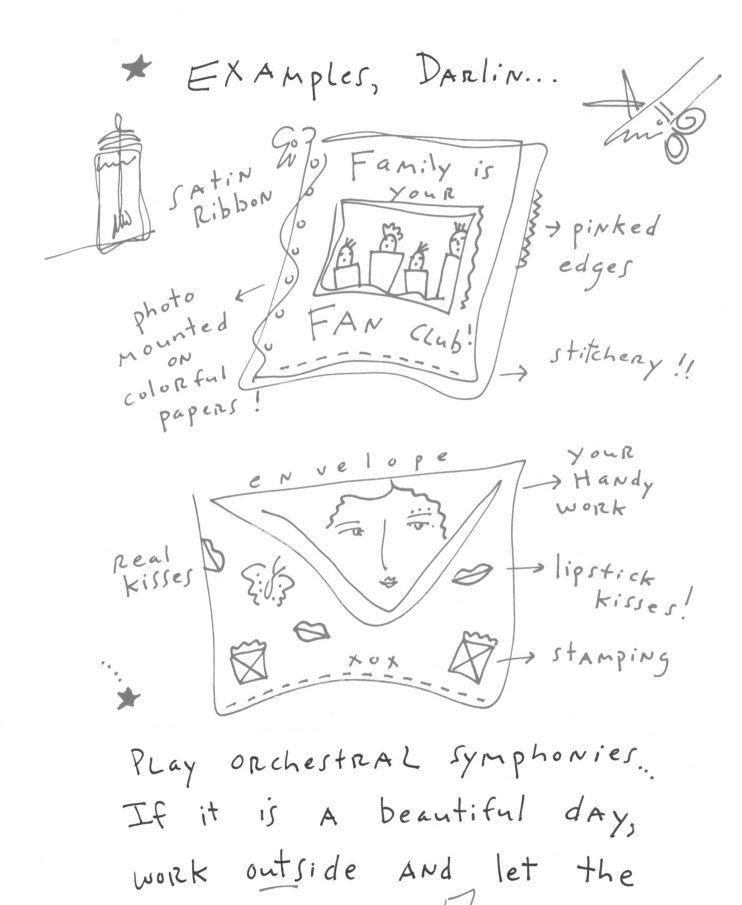

SATIN Ribbon

Family is your FAN Club!

→ pinked edges

photo mounted on colorful papers!

stitchery !!

→ your HANdy work

Real kisses

eNvelope

→ lipstick kisses!

→ stamping

XOX

PLAy oRchestRAL symphonies...
If it is A beautiful dAy,
woRk outside ANd let the

sun be your divine draft-
ing LAMP
and the ocean of BLue
skies your PLAYGROUND!
P.S. Think of using sweet
vintage valentines in a collage.
card!! Also... if you feel
pressured every Holiday Season
to pen a computerized Family
report... give yourself a gift
and do this with VERVE in
September or October... an
Autumn Love Note!

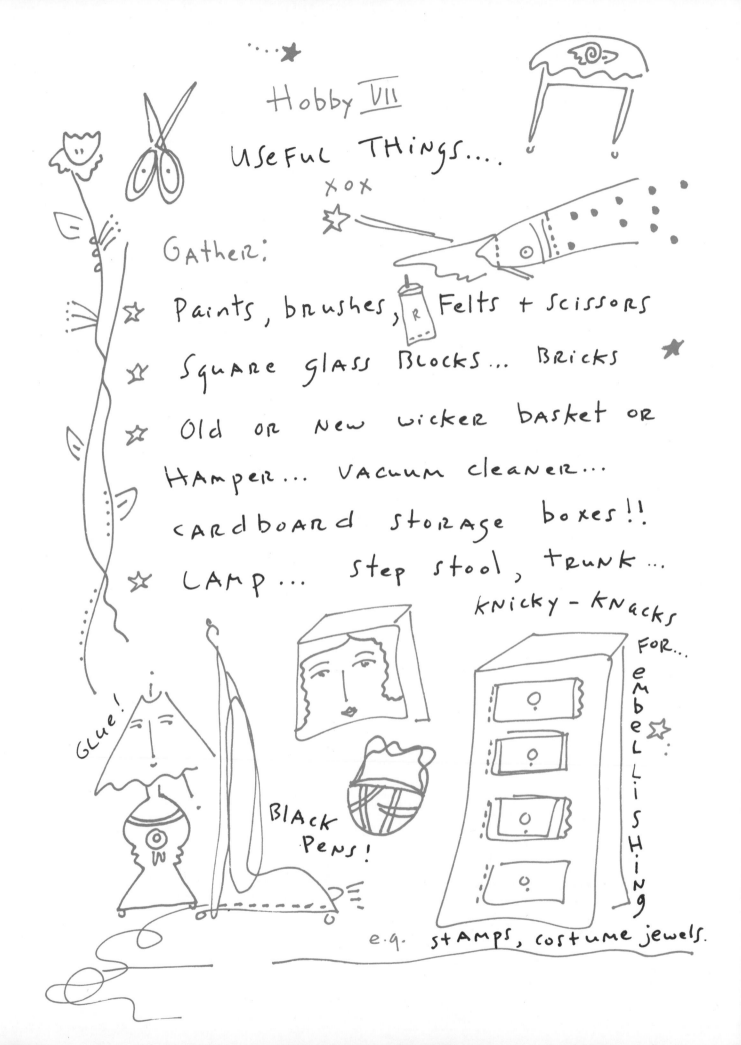

Hobby VII

Useful Things...

xox

Gather:

★ Paints, brushes, R Felts + scissors

★ Square glass Blocks... Bricks

★ Old or New wicker basket or Hamper... vacuum cleaner... cardboard storage boxes!!

★ Lamp... step stool, trunk...

Knicky - Knacks

For...

embellishing

Glue!

Black Pens!

e.g. stamps, costume jewels.

PRActicAl ANd oRdiNaRy THiNgs
ARe sweet coNfectioNs to youR
ARTFuL SpiRit!! They really

prefeR A life of DRAMA to
highfalutiN choRes (A bit like
us peRhaps!). TAke oN this
Hobby with A RebouNdiNg
Light-HeARtedNess.

      Simple glAss
blocks cAN be pAiNted ANd
used As bookeNds, sculptuRe,
oR dooRstops... It's best to
leAve some of the glass cleaR

for the play of light. Try
a series of faces with short
messages written in black pen.

common bricks offer the
same possibilities... Glue felt
to their bottoms... Pink edges!
Paint in abstract fashion
or detail a pretend town
where life is perfect !! Use
small brushes and take your

time [drawing]. Imagine a snowy night with a deep blue sky and cottage windows aglow in Van Gogh's buttery yellow. DRAW FROM WHAT IS A PERSONAL MEMORY BANK OF EXPERIENCES FELT AND LONGED FOR. Interpret life into a picture of symbols that are to an artist's language what words are to a writer. These symbols might be primeval or as intricate as a gently embroidered hanky from County Cork. PLAY WELL... PLAY FREE AND enjoy your WEALTH !! ☆ Next... with A larger brush, softly travel the woven texture of your wickery in A rainbow of colors. Let each visit dry A moment... so that the palette does not become muddy. If you love A shiny luster ... spray with A high- gloss polyurethane !!! P.S. let

Your BRUSH STROKES move like the tail of A SPRING KITE on A windy hillside....

Approach painting Theee VACUUM CLEANER in the SAME manner. Layers of swiftly moving colors... locked in A singular heart beat. Notice how mysterious it is to be lost, Alone with your Artful spirit.

in these moments that you

May FIND yourself... once again. Now, dolly, consider the ADORNMENT of cardboard storage boxes. I love the Antique versions covered in chintz wallpapers and would not dream of Altering their dignity. However, the MODERN versions Are FAiR gAme... Select those of interesting patterns And Add vintage postcards, lAdies' dress gloves, petite paper fans, plastic hair combs, and costume jewelry.

Oh yes... stage bills and any other personal essentials. (Small fabric pom-poms are nice as three-dimensional polka dots, too.)

Place this in your "dressing room" with a lovely LAMP dressed to match... Look! Finally... Rally a sturdy step stool or military trunk to take part in your COSMETIC surgery...

Find OLD Finial

Admit one

Pom-Poms

...of USEFUL THINGS....

let alone, re-cover, or paint on top!

add FRINGE + TAssels

Ribbon

Rick-RACK

coins

PAiNT, too!!

Small seAshells? or buttons!

LiFe's most NECESSARY Recipe:

Food

Clothing

New Yorker → great!

Shelter

ART

Time

ELViS

vinyl Records

78's

magazine covers!

USEFUL
GEMS....

GLASS
BLOCKS

← PAVING
BRICKS

P.S NEVER BE FOOLED BY ORDINARY
OBJECTS... IN YOUR HANDS they ARE
EXTRA-ORdiNAiRe.

Hobby VIII

PAPER Dolls... come Alive

For this project, plant your Artful Spirit deep inside the sanctuary created For High-Level Inspiration...

with your ART TREASURY at hand's Reach!!!

Include A Photo Album that offers those full-sized, semi-sticky pages.

This is

ART NEST

A dandy way to keep the dolls in order! Play the Broadway sound track from <u>Guys AND DOLLS</u>... brew A pot of <u>old</u>-fashioned cocoA... Real milk... FAT-FREE... AND

♪ Begin. ♪

decorate Album cover First

PAPYRus that DOLLS TALK AND tAlk AND tAlk...

By -------------

red

glue

EXAMPLE: DRAW... CUT.... PASTE... COLOR AS CRUDELY OR exactly AS YOUR VISION sees Fit.

MISS

SOPHIE

student

Tell A TALE OF Fact OR Folly.

EVERY dAY... she

MADE LIFe her wide-open CLASSROOM!!

ANother exAMPle... MORE specifically...

DRAW AND color!

→ Real photo FACE

clipped photo OF REAL Fish FROM A MAG!

H.

Cut shirt FROM Sunday Newspaper comics!

→ dRAW!

DRAW →

→ Felt

→ stitch

P.S. PAPER DOLLS CAN BE STATIONERY! think Love notes!

HOWARD WENT to HIS cHURCH every Sunday by the stReAM... ANd listened WELL.

IDEAS
FOR TALKING PAPYRUS
DOLLS...

do
with
kids
or
solo
...

CReate
AN
ENVIRON-
MENT ON
every page!

PLayful
CHARACTER DEVELOPMENT!!

Hobby IX

"Oh, dear OFFICE... you are
really very small, just Big enough
...For Love... that's ALL"
Aunt Pearl

Collect from your Art Treasury...
Paints, markers... glue, felts...shoe
box... buttons, scissors, Velcro,
pinking shears... yarns.

Size is no barrier to
creating a Home away from

Home that wraps your Artful

spirit in an all-embracing...

"I CAN DO THIS...NOT ONLY WELL!!
...But
...BEAUTIFULLY AND LIKE NO

OTHER!"

PERSONALIZE this fertile territory of NOBLE WORK with HANDMADE reminders of your MANTRA:

"MY Cup... is RARELY half Full... ALWAYS cresting... NEVER resting."

Let's begin with dolling up your throne... by fashioning A CHAIR "PLAQUE" that will RALLY... task AFTER task. YOU MAY wish to do A suite of them AND change AS often AS you do LIPSticks!

Cut A living (biomorphic) shape of fabric... If you are timid at sewing, use pinking shears for A finished edge!! The material should have some Body... e.g., CANVAS OR felt. Then design AN image with or with-out words. Be A bit cryptic or NOt. Fuss with trims and paints and pens... Use Velcro to Attach or tie with Ribbons or RICKRACK...

Look...

...to the back of your chair for All to see!

BRAVO!!

rosebud→

RANDOM buttons

crocheted doily

PAINT AND PEN work!

...📷 Other titles!!

"Popping my Buttons is NOT AN Option Today"

" INTERRUPTIONS WELCOME... "

" CREATIVE Power Station I "

" ENJOY... EMPLOY THE Process "

" MANY mountains ARE invisible... with sky blue peaks of TRUTH... Sweet TRUTH "

Next... transform that dull shoe box into your DESK ANGEL... Place her in a corner for 24-hour duty...

→ ribbon

→ YARNS

Real photo or drawn ←

RELAX

collage, cut And paste

Real Fabric

OFFICE

HEROES ARE SELF-made ...daily

felt glued to card-board

And finally... consider planting a cork strip in sight where snippets of ART can parade in the office wind like fresh linens hung out for an April sun to dry. Whip up FAVE characters and string from RICKRACK...... or sweet love notes...

Stan

Pat

A CAST OF PALS!

xoxo

mom... Hurry back Home to ME!!

Hobby X

PILLOW MAGIC

Some of us collect Limoges, Fiesta Ware, and beach glass. I collect Pillows!! For this hobby you will need: Old or new fabrics, paints, pens, glue, trims, stuffing and/or ready-made Pillows, scissors, buttons... metal button forms, photos!

This project applauds the brave mind-set of mixing and matching Patterns, Colors, textures...

in an effort to not only set a comfy home but to excite the eye. For example, perhaps you are in Love with lipstick RED and Palm Beach Yellow... Living with four walls of both may be tooo much.. yes?? However, a few cushy pillows will work by including their VERVE, politely. The love I espouse for extending those lives of FINERY... comes

from a visit to a Boston
Millinery on Beacon Hill... while
in college. There... resting
in a lovely window... sat a
paisley silk TURBAN that spoke
the following to me... Gentility,
comfort... beauty... and Romantic
dreams come true!! Upon my
entering, the sales woman
reluctantly removed theee
hat and stood guard while
I tried it on, EVEN though

FRies... salad
caesar
anne
me?

it was snug and BEYOND
expensive by my waitress
standards. I exchanged the
tip money of $68.50 that
was promised to next week's
bills back in Ann Arbor. The
hat box was carried onto
the plane... and years later,
after being worn only a few
times — VERy Few (there is
No Ritz Carlton in Niles!)
Theee Hat became A

DUE
NOW...
tuition
books
phone

135.

Round, happily transformed pillow! Perfect for a dainty boudoir chair! ...This magical Hobby can recycle fabrics that hold dear meaning in your life's sojourn... Sooo before you bear gifts to GOOD WILL... hold on to that BRIDES-maid's gown, Aunt Pearl's Christmas hanky, or NANNA's tweed cape with the velvet trim... THINK Pillows, doll!

136.

... CARRY ON viscerally confident

AND play with the possibilities!

ZICKRACK
OR HAND
stitching!

Antique
Buttonry

& store-
bought...

dAMASK,
linen...

patterned
OR MMM...
PLAIN JANE!

cut AND collage felts AND
velvets... ACCESSORize with rosebuds, pearls, old crystal
beads... EMBELLISH!

CONSider covering metal button
forms in vintage swatches of
embroidery... these may serve

...well as a bucolic Reminder of slower days... Garden-side! With floss and needle in hand... TUFFets away from Lazy-Boy Recliners!!

More ideas... xox

Devote a luxurious pillow to a collection of WELL-CRAFted jewelry! Pins of Substance!

wear when needed!

A MESSENGER Pillow!

scribe from inner chambers

MAY SWEET PEACE... BE HOMEMADE HERE

xoxoxoxoxoxoxoxox

the DiME-store Pillow!!

think!! teeNy! kitschy!

collect your FAVORite dolls AND trinkets... glue or stitch oN!!

FABRiC FROM 9Rade school uniFoRM!

PHoto tribute...

Kind... dear, Good... HAZEL

→Actual impression oN FabRic — cut PRofile to fit... Add D E T A i L s !

trims

Hand Paint...

SAiL   FRee

Bring iN the FAmily gANg ANd create PERsoNAL CANVASES!!

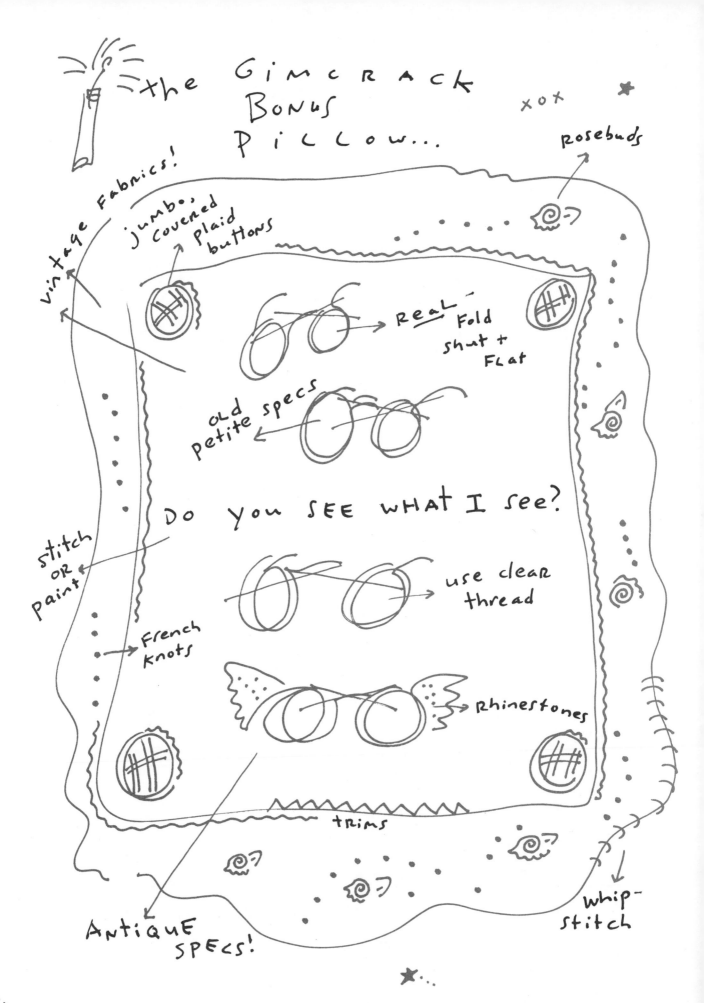

the GIMCRACK
BONUS
PILLOW...

xox

rosebuds

vintage Fabrics!

Jumbo, covered plaid buttons

REAL-
Fold
shut +
Flat

old petite specs

DO YOU SEE WHAT I SEE?

stitch
or
paint

use clear thread

French knots

Rhinestones

trims

ANTIQUE SPECS!

whip-stitch

ON EARTH... MAterial INventions oFten Render sweet truths... study Buttons!!! Those self-Reliant icons of lives well spent. Holding together the calico wrappings of pioneering Scouts, these chipper chips of pearly shells And plastic deserve our Reverence and, I may say, our attention!! Sometimes what they hold together is Not of Flaxen fabric but of all that stands to sway time's threatening chant... Fast asleep. Fast Asleep. Forever... we long to button up our best of dreams and schemes!!

☆..

Bonus...

Button Bracelet...

...make a zillion and never shop for another generic gift!

aunt pearl's..
1968
nice
odds and bits

→ Take gold- or silver-toned safety pins and add buttons or beads... at random intervals

THEN

Take elastic (a snappy metallic is nice) and

jumbo

using two rows, one at top and. one at bottom - WEAVE together... tie ends in Knots and

☆

PRESTO- magnifico!!

a CUFFED JEWEL is BORN!

Hobby XI

washbasin

Sleepers... But keepers...
F o u n d   O b j e c t s ...xox

Remember. Adventure V and

gather: Old Suitcase, clock, TV...

metal fan, basin... windows, glass

plates, dividing screen... paneled

door... And Naturally your ART

T R E A S U R Y.

Knowing how we
all love to READ
and TALK and
especially... BE
understood... you
will FAVOR this hobby!

143.

These sleepy gems are ready for your ARTFul SPIRIT to smarten and be of great service... ☆ Soul SERVICE!!

★ First, the genuine symbol of travel... OR the carrying of REAL and invisible Baggage!? TAKE A suitcase AND snap it to full Attention with PAINTING AND COLLAGING, AND charting A MAP of MESSAGES! No time for... sporting

that NON secret Victoria's
bikini on the isle of Nevis?
...IN REAL LIFE...
It's braces for little suzie
or a plane ticket to sur-
prise mom on her 70th birth-
day... wherever!!! your life
is pinpointed, for now...
in many mysterious ways,
WE ARE perpetually traveling!!
Sooo... dolly, muster a living
map to Guide... your Compass and
ALL!

Touch all sides...

BEND like a NON-WEEPING Willow...
Laugh like A NEWBORN...
AND DREAM A
Cinderella DREAM FOR ME...
XOX

Private, PORTABLE BILLBOARDS...

NORTH   South
UP OR DOWN...
EVERY single day...let your worries out FOR RECESS!

MMM...

The next doozie-doodle!!!

Give CPR to a waveless television set and enjoy its new Attitude!!

Next... doctor this profound icon
Of absolutely no flexibility...YET!
LOOK, darlin... the CLOCK
it is! AND in this case

Big is Better... Huge is best...

RELAX OR PERISH

paint
AND
Festoon
with
buttons
AND
coins
on
sides!

ANY
old
time-
piece
will
do!

Mercy

you decide!?

RUMMAGE your A.T.... TRY A FRESH twist!
(ART TREASURY)

14c.

Another provincial bit of history, eager to TANGO ♪♪ with MODERNITY is the FAN.. one with nice visible propellers. Instead of sending your message off in a bottle by sea... pen it by land...

NICE is not A WEAKNESS

Row your very own Boat

FAN ALL WORRY... FAR, FAR Away

elevate your original invention

xox

FOR ALL to SEE..!!

And now, dolly, let's give an old metal basin a new career. Even a lost lid will do... Over one recent summer my sister kathy needed to let her up-north pals know when she was NAPPING.. So she gave voice to the flip side of an enameled Bucket... It READS...

vio-let

Red trim

white

Hush now, pleeez...sweet dreams need time to PLAY

And

it hangs beside her screen door above a flowering box of geraniums... AS NEEded! GLASS PLAtes are very eager players in your heart's desire to TALK in colors, shapes, and textures.

Try old, tinted, or newly frosted... Combine your paints with paper collaging or Not...

The only parochial discipline

you may need throughout this Renaissance is to <u>VA</u>Ry... mix... your use of materials. Sometimes you might wish to <u>ONLY</u> PAiNt... <u>ONLY</u> DRAW... and give your glue gun and Faux Bijoux A Holiday!

WHOA!!

PLACE NEAR SUNLight, dolly

OR bACK iN FELt And RESt lazily!

P.S. use paints designed for glass

Finally... tackle the _still,_ wide-open prairies of a paneled window or door. Take advantage of its individual character in its shapes and territorial moldings... Actually _use_ these or prop up as top-notch DECLARATIONS!

J   to

o   you

y   dolly

DO NOT FEAR NEWNESS!

Hobby XII

...A sweet and zesty... Photo-Story Book

Even if you are one of the well-ritualized souls that has kept every lock of baby hair, first tooth, and honor-roll report card ... this is a new hobby for you. If you are one of many more who plunge into boxed stacks of parched photos, stored basement

IN forgettable places, this
hobby will save you from
all past guilt... for not being
more mechanized!!

Before there were
photo albums, there were
years and years of lovingly
made "SCRAP" BOOKS. Often
they were A core of stiff
black pages with A grand
cover... filled with keepsakes...

Not necessarily in any order or theme. Let's weave a bit of modern magic with the inspiration of this old concept as our muse. For this hobby you will need:

☆ definitely the Art Treasury!!

☆ Assorted Acid-Free papers, if possible, and exquisite papers of different natures.

☆ A group of meaningful photos and keepsakes.

movie
gone with the wind
xox

prom 1944

Take time to gather the latter... the more the better!! Your life is worth volumes, isn't that so, dolly? Begin with decorating the cover... contemplate its title. It should Fit your sensibilities.

Rosettes

ribbons

Row Row Row Your Boat... gen t ly through Rough And silky waters... LiFe is but A dreAm

use photos

HAnd Scribe

The soul and heart of
this book can be made
visible not just by pictures
but by the scripting of
specific memories or feelings
that these photos ignite.

Write ALL without pause

directly upon the pages or in

A separate letter that can

be placed in an envelope and

affixed to the page of note.

Look →

pinked edges!

summer 1956
CAMP Hayowentah

1967
christmas

dear...
memories

→ glue
tied bow
And lace to
envelope,
so that it
is secure...

What is perfect About this

hobby is that, like A MiRRoR,

it will tell you again what

you know to be true, And

more. Yes, darlin, you CAN

go back because once you've

traveled via Life's map...

All is owned for now

and tomorrow. Select your

BEST TRIPS and exalt them!!

How?? By simply Remembering

the colors, fragrances, images,

and ultimately the Feelings

that washed your dreams

and schemes into a story

that only you can call your

OWN. Appoint these to A handmade   castle of
wonder... And return often!!

Categorized or Not, it is
All A REMARKable journey...
And one in PROGRESS!!!
Is it Not?   xox

       P.S. If you Are A
caregiver, this hobby is A
balm to those who have
"stalled" so to speak, in their
sojourn. This hobby can

REMEDY them like no prescrip-
tion medicine on the market
today!! Become A personal
historian and create A
type of illustrated journal...
Guide them and NUDGE
them to speak of the past
"Good Times"... even encourage
them to draw or color without
R E S E R V A t i o N !!!

Lemon
orange

MRS. I. Potter

Remember...

...some passports do not come in the mail... they are yours the day you are born, to both worlds... those visible and invisible...

Travel richly and far,

[dolly!]

...and keep a sweet and zesty photo-story book!!

Hobby XIII

A Family Collage...
Mission Statement!

All you will need, dolly, is
canvas OR paper and... your
Art Treasury!!

Photos

This hobby is as sweet

as a Brown Betty on the 4th

of July and a SNAP to do.

The lovingly made Art... A

REAL Family Collaboration, can

be done on stretched canvas

or paper! Frame the finished

piece with colorful molding or glued RICKRACKS or ... pop into Plexiglas frames!!

First... call a family meeting and use your chitchat list (next page) to gather ideas and the words to spell out your very personal Purpose... as a petite "Nation" under one Roof! Make this an intimate "tea party" for those you love theee Most!!

kids!

"CHITCHAT"

FAMILY IDEAS FOR...
MISSION statement...

★ GOALS... Hopes... dreams

★ PAST LESSONS...

★ FORGIVENESS...

★ RULES FOR DIFFERENCES OF
OPINION !!.

★ There is NO "I" in the
word "TEAM"...

★ Daily doses of Humor!

Fido

Then, share older and current photos... plus the tools of your Art Treasury to build a collage of pictures and words. Perhaps it will look a bit like this...

PAINT

CANVAS

My FAMily 'tis of theee...
We LOVE each other BIG
TiMe

REAL photo

As you can surely see!

→ Rick-Rack border

→ YARN

Colored Felt Marker

→ FELT

P.S.
FRAgile...

Colored PAPER

button

HANDLE ALL HEARTS with CARE

You may wish to create several pieces over time... And dedicate a PRIMO wall in a well - trafficked area... As a FRESH REMINDER for one and all. Think, too, of gifting miniatures OF these to those family members who are dear and NOT so NEAR!! If they ARE raising a young brood, it just might become a golden map... second time around !!

* xox *

Home sweet ★..NEST...

sample "WALL"

for mission statements...

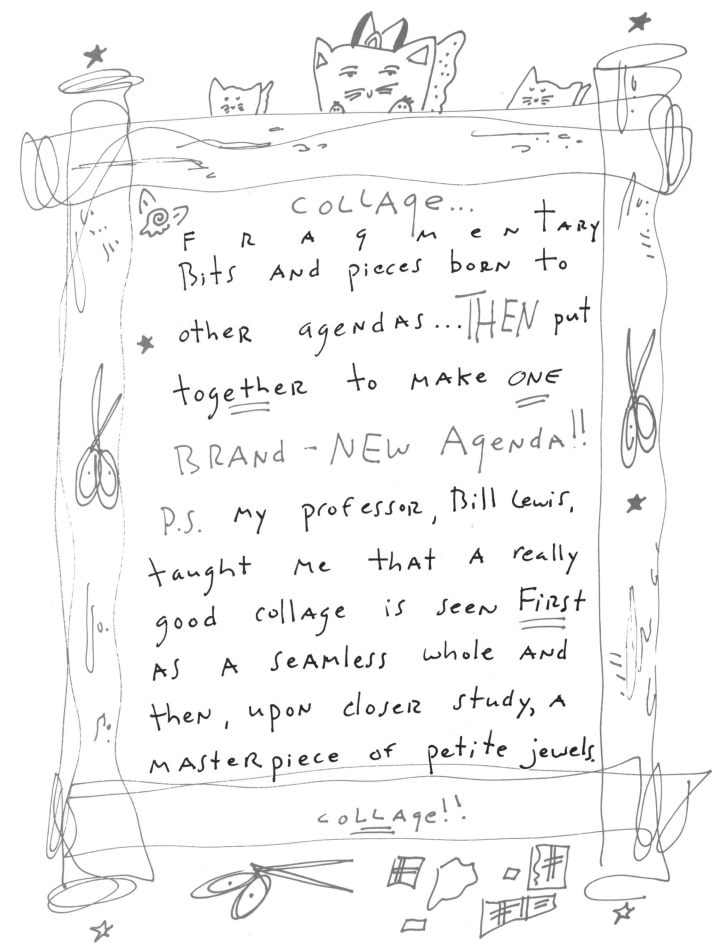

COLLAGE...
FRAGMENTARY
Bits AND pieces born to
other agendas...THEN put
together to MAKE ONE
BRAND-NEW Agenda!!
P.S. My professor, Bill Lewis,
taught me that A really
good collage is seen FIRST
AS A SEAMLESS whole AND
then, upon closer study, A
MASTERpiece of petite jewels.

COLLAGE!!

Aunt Pearl's Favorite Hobby..... of All Time! xoxo

Every day, like a master WEAVER.... tatting small talk with Big talk!!! Study your conversations, darlin. They Feed the ARtFul SPirit for good or ill...

Hobby XIV

Mini - tattlers... Book-
marks, Auto ornaments, etc.
(fetch your ★ Art treasury)
Without a doubt our eyes
long to read messages!! No
matter where, when, or how
they are penned. It is our
code of unspoken conversations.
You, darlin, can
create a quiet chat with
yourself that, like a cup
of tea or bowl of chicken

gumbo... FORTifies iN tiny
doses! All you will Need
for this hobby REALLY is A
Nicely sorted - out bAtch
of youR thoughts And
Access to A pRiNt shop. you
know, A local, speedy one!!
This source will offer heavy
cARd stocks, colorful inks, copies,
And lAminAtion, so that
you may plAy with the

following PERSONAL DIALOGUES!

my own preference is to

PEN All words iN my own

handwriting... however, type-

setting in diFFERENT FONTS

is AN option! Perhaps

mixing both is A fine com-

promise. Remember, too, that

these mini-tattlers ARE

A good way to "tALk" to

pAls... And FAmiLy!!

Bookmarks...!!! use both sides... Vary sizes, Add color or perhaps A dried Flower from your... country Powwow!!

Laminate!

Always Read between the words

stitch edges in A cheery Floss from the Artful Treasury!

Add life with water-colors or felt-tip pens!

Tv is For Sissies

I Must RELAX

Borrow wisdom

126.

It is possible to work to scale or, if you wish, a jumbo approach... The print shop can easily reduce your art to fit into a smaller bookmark fashion. Creating on a larger, more open scale affords you a nice playground for words and illustration... See my playground on the next page...

Add A
Ribbon
through
punched
hole.

x o x o x o

secret

LiFe is AN
UNFOLDiNG
L o v e
L e t t e R...
full
of P R o m i s e.

OPEN
AND
READ
WELL

Real
Posy

cut
A Flowing shApe! oR dRAw borders!

Now that you understand

this EASY AND NATURAL hobby...

let's look At Auto ORNAMENTS!

Much in the same mode

As plush dice or pine tree

Air fresheners, you CAN

whip up A lovely collection

of mini-tAttlers. They

CAN either dAngle or rest

carefully in your view ...

180.

WHEN SNUG AT HOME, PLANT ANOTHER BATCH OF SNIPPETS WHERE YOU VISIT OFTEN... INSIDE YOUR CLOSET DOOR, MEDICINE CABINET, OR CUTLERY DRAWER! EVEN ON YOUR WASHER - DRYER !! CHANGE THESE AS THE SEASONS DANCE A NEW FOLLY !!

I'll BET YOU WILL BE AMAZED AT THE WELLSPRING OF WORDS

And pictures just waiting inside you... waiting to become mini-tattlers freshly laminated by your local print shop! What wonderful conversations there will be!! xox

Some of the Best Hobbies
for your ARTFul Spirit...
ARe those Not seen by one
and All... posted to a wall.
Let the Moonbeams in your
Eyes win the Prize!!

You ARE A FiNE Hobby... dear one.

PRiNCE
CHARM-
LESS
HAS
LeFt
the
Building

SEARCH High... NOT LOW, FOR
MR. TRUE LOVE, DARLIN!!

Hobby XV

THE ... "I most certainly DO
want to be in Love"
Hobby

This is cupid's best tonic for
all of those in search of Mr.
or Mrs. Almost - Right. Many
times the LOVE-SAFARI zigs and
zags into wild jungles that
at first appear lush with
promise and ALAS prove to be
riddled with monstrous follies.
If those junkets have

filled your suitcase with souvenirs of

WOE.... PROCEED, darlin. All this

hobby will need is a journal

(or volumes) either handmade

from PAPERS of character or a

dolled-up store-bought one...

And pens to tell your TALes....

(color and illustrate as you

go along). Begin by making

an outline as an indexed map...

yes, dolly, of your Heart...

L   K

example!

Index

1966 Robert Stone... high school, Brother Rice. (horrible kisser)

1968 Jeffery Burns... Freshman, U. of M. (wild, preppy boozer)

1969 Stewart Bartlett... Freshman, Jeffery's best friend, U. of M. (Rhodes Scholar)

1970 John Platt... sophomore, Kendall Art Institute (Picasso Fan)

1973 Bill Avondale, professor at Eastern Tech, (married, sort of) Full of Huge plans for later.

1975 Dr. Evan Pierce... psychologist at Free clinic (needy and poor)

1982 ... keep Remembering and writing + reading

Add photos!

★ Every bizee heart needs a spring cleaning now and then

As you record this directory..
try and sift through the fog
and find the lessons that sit
beside the pain. Let go of blame
and the oh-so-tedious search
for understanding. Just restore
your best vision, as a child
might look upon a bright BLUE
day and see so clearly its
majesty. Say..." Perhaps John
was a this and a that... but
my time with him taught me
to stand firm and question

parts of me that even I had forgotten." Antique yarns of failed loves spin from generation to generation as a steely CPR for one's HEART... OF HEARTS. saying through different dramas... "you are not stupid or a lost moonbeam. HURTS are often born like the fuzzy, scooching caterpillar... And can take flight as a lovely And wiser Butterfly... So Free, you'll SEE."

where true love awaits you...

AFter journaling your heart's expeditions and the hidden treasures they have bestowed... Build a chapter of EXODUS that gives you a FRESH pass-port to those lands that are truly lush with the kind of Romance that lasts solar Heart ♡ Beats from now. In this chapter, cite the specifics that warrant such a Fine union...

Prepare to go again?

★ You know, darlin... define Realistic, High expectations!!!

And REMEMBER this...

Nothing your HEART
has gifted is ever,
ever... wasted,
only wisdom
e a r n e d.

LIFE is ALL About...
Beginning Again

And
Again
And
Again,
dolly.

true
ROMANCE
Awaits
you.
Believe it!

Hobby XVI

"I AM *ENORMOUSLY IN LOVE... FOR keeps"

This is AN intimate hobby.

Please have your Art Treasury

on call for the making of

A book or independent pages!

Today and tomorrow you are

A

POET:

one who displays beauty of

thought, language, etc., in

expression.

—Webster's

INK

Before you envelop your imagination in the poetic process of scribing on paper what your heart knows to be true, use this outline:

I love _____ with a passion deeper and broader than the GRAND CANYON........ Because...

Making preliminary notes is
like preparing fine ingredients
for a delicate recipe. In
order to create the whole,
one must take care and gather
the inseparable fragments
that constitute a multi-layered
work of ART. Your one true
LOVE, put to paper, is a
heavenly soufflé of JOY
Once you have prepared...
settle into a deep solitude,

195.

where piano music halts all
interruption and you are
free to sculpt the invisible
into our world. Support
your poetry with drawings and
colored washes!! Make a
copy and give the original
to your best mate on earth...
This is fair, darlin, because
the first DRAFT is engraved
forever in the glorious chambers
of your Heart !!!

LIFE'S MYSTERIOUS SCREENPLAY... HOW ART CAN become a soothing, SELF-MADE BALM FOR HEARTache.

Not sold in stores or on television...

YOUR VERY OWN tool-box

wow... well, I simply I had no idea...

63

A PATCH of PAIN CAN be HANdled with GRACE **IF** your Life is ARtFuL!! How so, you wonder? Well, let's look At the Ritual of cookery that is put in FuLL Motion when A loss happens. Strangers became instant friends of the family in the preparing

...eggs...

casseroles and powdered

cakes. Busy hands... fussing

with unrelated ingredients...

make for a HEALING

Feast!

tuNA
Noodle

uncle
SAL

what a great guy... please pass the...

CREAtive Acts ARE First

A MiRACLE OF PROCESS...

SECOND, A GiFt to BeHOLd.

199.

EXAMPLE

①. OF HOW THIS WORKS:

HARRIET DEALS with
HEARTACHE by escaping
to the Movies And power
shopping.
¢
MERCY... Not
Feeling much
better At All...   No, Sir.

②
                                  XOXO

CHRISTINE deals with
HEARTACHE by having A
NIAGARA FALLS CRY, PENNING
in her JOURNAL, And skipping
WAVES At the beach...
Later she
paints A
portrait of
her "Disposition"   She's
                         better!

200.

POOOR

Harriet missed the process... ✱

And has nothing to behold

but a credit card bill, WHILE

Christine has the joy of

personal Expression... PLUS

the handmade ARt that

✱

Mirrors her sweet, wounded

♡heart, Trying to SELF-HEAL

Sooo, dolly, when we

were made... long before man

invented miracles of INSTANT

Remedy ... AN invisible SOLAR

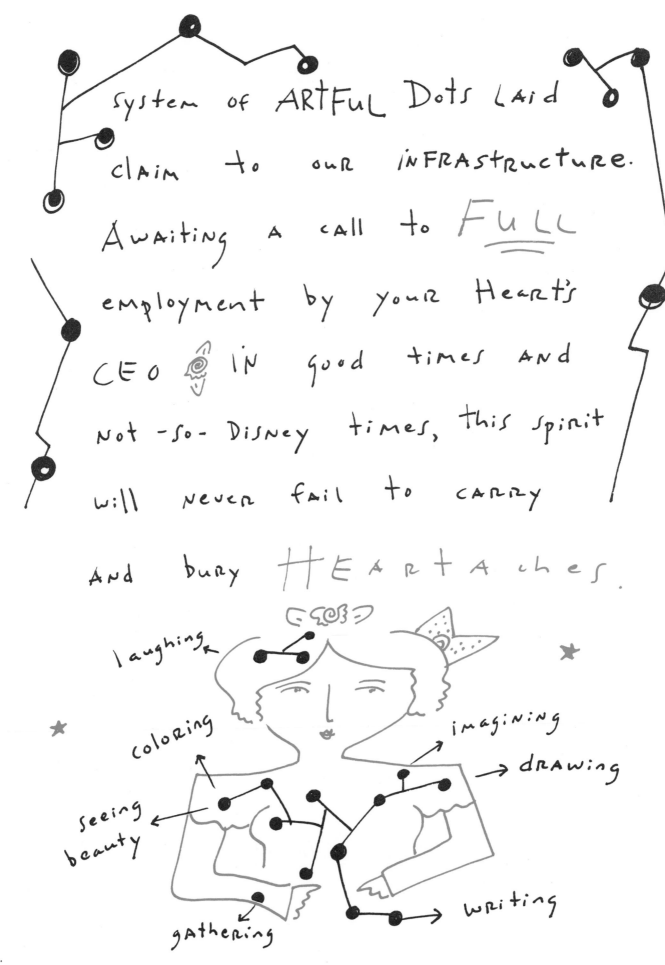

System of ARTFuL Dots LAid claim to our INFRAstructure. Awaiting a call to FULL employment by your Heart's CEO IN good times And Not-so-Disney times, this spirit will never fail to carry And bury HEARTAches.

laughing

coloring

seeing beauty

gathering

imagining

drawing

writing

Hobby XVII

this too will pass... A SELF-gifting Hobby for the deeply BROKEN HEARTED ☾

Early this morning I awoke before my body told me to, because my mind had just screened one ELM-Street HORRIFIC nightmare! The kind that you fight to escape by opening your SANDMAN eyes and reciting A ROSARY of Lightning Hail Marys in thanks and A plea for Future MERCY. For some, there are

very Real Nightmares that do
not cease as Readily. God bless
and envelop you TIGHT like a
cashmere bunting might if it came
in EXTRA-LARge xoxo! Let this
hobby be my lullaby to your
heart... Rest a bit and listen...

Find...

your Art treasury

hot Real cocoa

writing paper and envelopes

a stretched CANVAS

Airmail

COCOA

Begin by penning a flood of Letters to... "whom it may concern." Speak your Heartache Loud and Clear in a private silence. Do as many as it takes to help sweep the soot away. Cleanse each and every Chamber of your Heart so that the un-wanted Renter "PAIN" flees sooner than tomorrow. Sign and date each letter, then store

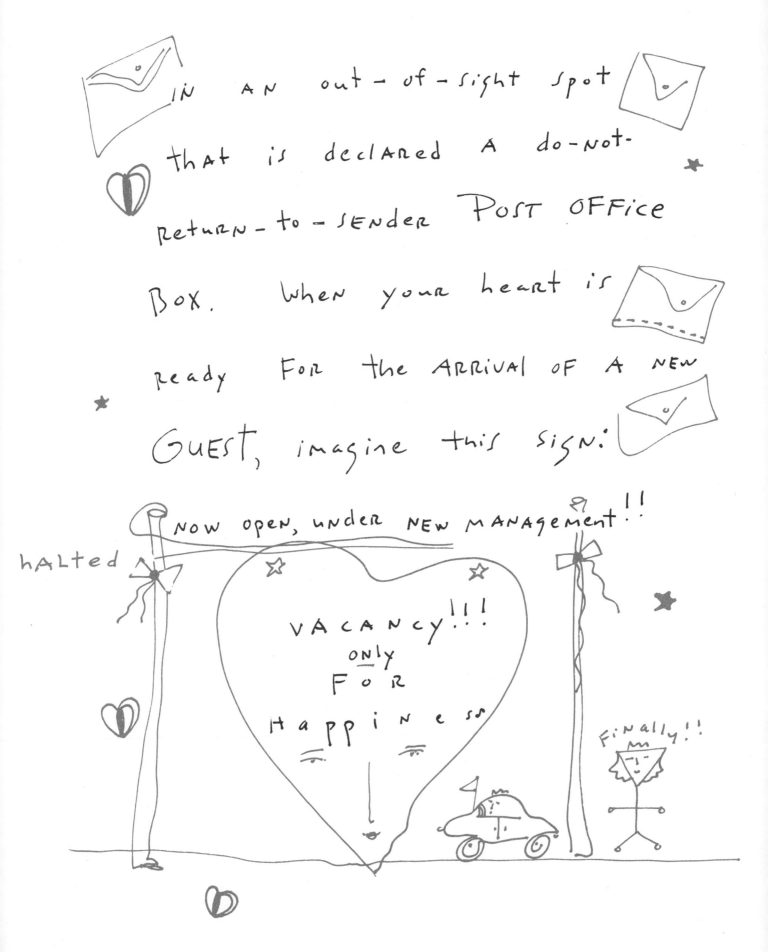

IN AN out-of-sight spot that is declared A do-not-return-to-sender POST OFFICE BOX. When your heart is ready FOR the ARRIVAL OF A NEW GUEST, imagine this sign:

NOW OPEN, UNDER NEW MANAGEMENT!!

hALTed

VACANCY!!!
ONLY FOR
H a p p i n e s s

FiNally!!

As you welcome this new RENTER, plant a picture garden on canvas for the world to see. Include the different hybrids of joy that ALWAYS come back to you after long winters and nippy springs... Call them by name, darlin...

use photos, too!

P.S. perhaps they were always bloomin your tuckered glimmers just couldn't see.

collage away!

dad

MOM

1949

XMAS

"Let's PLAY HOOKY CAMP"

mitt

mag

the beach

ANNA

We, as artful spirits, are not of one gift... we are beings that come with more than we can ever spend wisely in our life's short spell. When we are openly wide eyed to the "possibilities" before us, next to us... beside us, and within us, those gifts fall like a star-burst of diamonds upon our velvet skies.

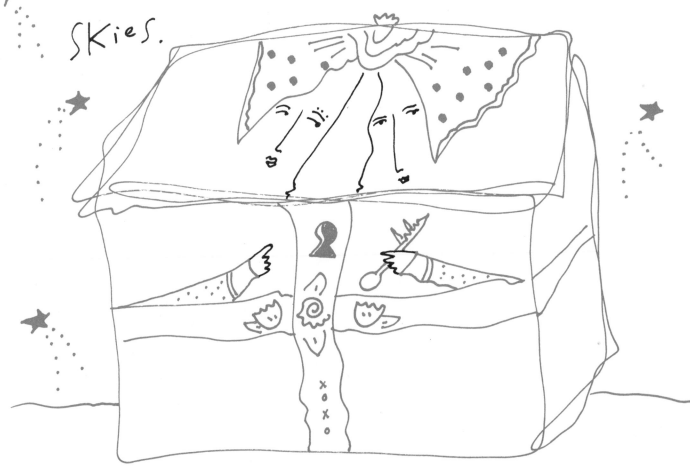

you, my darling,
have the power
to make beauty,
truth, and love
visible....
call upon your
Artful
Spirit
to assist you
daily!!
And when
the landscape
looks bare,
Look...
sweet angel...
Look
Again.
Love,
Aunt Pearl
1999

Index

to reach
Nancy...
1-800-776-3739

FAX NANCY
AT
1·616·683·9344

website info: www.therealnancydrew.com